Boats

by
Gail Saunders-Smith

Pebble Books

an imprint of Capstone Press

Pebble Books

Pebble Books are published by Capstone Press
151 Good Counsel Drive, P.O. Box 669, Mankato, Minnesota 56002
http://www.capstone-press.com

022010 5652VMI

Library of Congress Cataloging-in-Publication Data
Saunders-Smith, Gail.
    Boats / by Gail Saunders-Smith.
    p. cm.—(Transportation)
    Summary: Photographs and simple text introduce the reader to many types of
boats and ships, including canoes, paddle wheels, and aircraft carriers.
    ISBN-13: 978-1-56065-497-1 (hardcover)
    ISBN-10: 1-56065-497-X (hardcover)
    ISBN-13: 978-1-56065-968-6 (softcover pbk.)
    ISBN-10: 1-56065-968-8 (softcover pbk.)
    1. Boats and boating—Juvenile literature. [1. Boats and boating. 2. Ships.]
I. Title. II. Series.
    VM150.S325 1997
    623.8—dc21   97-23583

Editorial Credits
Lois Wallentine, editor; Timothy Halldin and James Franklin, design;
Michelle L. Norstad, photo research

Photo Credits
International Stock/Peter Langone, cover
Mark Turner, 10
Unicorn Stock/H.H. Thomas, 8; Karen Holsinger Mullen, 12;
    Alice M. Prescott, 1, 16
U.S. Navy, 20
Valan Photos/Phil Norton, 4; Tom W. Parkin, 6; Jean Bruneau, 14
George White Location Photography, 18

Table of Contents

A canoe is a boat.
It can work on a river.

A kayak is a boat.
It can work on a river.

A paddle wheeler is a boat. It can work on a river.

A sailboat is a boat.
It can work on a lake.

A rowboat is a boat.
It can work on a lake.

A motorboat is a boat.
It can work on a lake.

A tugboat is a boat.
It can work on the ocean.

A cruise ship is a ship.
It works on the ocean.

An aircraft carrier is a ship. It works on the ocean.

Words to Know

aircraft carrier—a large, flat ship where airplanes and jets can land

canoe—a small, shallow boat that people move through water with paddles

cruise ship—a large ship that people travel on for a vacation

kayak—a small, enclosed boat for one person

motorboat—a fast, medium-sized boat that is moved by a motor

paddle wheeler—a large riverboat that is moved by a spinning wheel

rowboat—a small boat that people move through water with oars

sailboat—a small or large boat that moves by catching wind in its sails

tugboat—a small, powerful boat that pulls or pushes ships

Read More

Asimov, Isaac and Elizabeth Kaplan. *How Do Big Ships Float?* Ask Isaac Asimov. Milwaukee: Gareth Stevens Publishing, 1993.

Davies, Kay and Wendy Oldfield. *My Boat.* Milwaukee: Gareth Stevens Publishing, 1994.

Lincoln, Margarette. *Amazing Boats.* Eyewitness Juniors. New York: Alfred A. Knopf, 1992.

Internet Sites

Do you want to find out more about boats? Let FactHound, our fact-finding hound dog, do the research for you.

Here's how:

1) Visit *http://www.facthound.com*

2) Type in the **Book ID** number: **156065497X**

3) Click on **FETCH IT**.

FactHound will fetch Internet sites picked by our editors just for you!

Note to Parents and Teachers

The Transportation series supports national social studies standards related to transportation. This book describes and illustrates various types of boats and ships. The book also introduces three different bodies of water. The photographs support early readers in understanding the text. The repetition of words and phrases helps early readers learn new words. This book also introduces early readers to subject-specific vocabulary words, which are defined in the Words to Know section. Early readers may need assistance to read some words and to use the Table of Contents, Words to Know, Read More, Internet Sites, and Index/Word List sections of the book.

Index/Word List

Word Count: 100
Early-Intervention Level: 6